Heavy like Heaven

Lauren Zulinski

BookLeaf Publishing

Presentation by *BookLeaf Publishing*

Web: www.bookleafpub.com

E-mail: info@bookleafpub.com

ISBN: 9789357210423

First edition 2022

DEDICATION

To my sweet girl. You are so loved Sabrina Grace.

Heavy, Like Heaven

I don't believe in heaven.
But, heaven is a fire
built in a stove
burning
on the other side of infinity
field -barren and dark,
that stretches farther
away, the closer
you get.

Heaven is heaviness
in the heart
- yearning
for a warmth
you wish you had.
Heaven is a weight
upon the soul.
Like a dumbbell, caving
in the back
of your throat.
The inevitable choking out
of an unattainable
desire.

I don't believe in souls.
But souls are the part of us

that can’t be touched,
bought, or held down.
Souls are the wild horse,
untamed beauty.
Souls are nasty-willful
Defiance, struttin’ it’s stuff
‘round the second-floor hallway
of the intermediate school,
like it’s “the shit”.
But don’t you even think
about sending it to the office!
Yeah, heaven is pretty hard
on a soul.

There are so many things
in which I don’t believe,
that I wonder
if my life isn’t built
on a lack.
If this isn’t “what I get”
for not making more
with the time that I’ve had.
As if the hole
in my belly could be filled
by belief
alone.

Somewhere, in a womb,
there’s a fire

in a stove
- a movement in the dark
a speck on a machine.
And in that someplace,
it's okay if you don't believe
in heaven,
because it's inside you,
so call it what you
will.
And it's fine if you don't
know about souls,
because the fire in your belly
doesn't know
about them either.

But when you find out,
you will teach her,
in whatever form that she arrives,
that heaven is the heaviest
Of all Things.
And even if you don't believe
in a place, nestled in cloud,
where the dead are reunited,
and everything is perfect,
so what?
Because real heaven
hurts like hell.
And when one fire dies,
the truest believers

cry their eyes out…
then, light another.

The Earth Turned, and we all Stood Still

I sometimes confuse
dreams with reality
- a movie seen once,
in early morning.
The lingering storm
of grey matter
dancing on my
cells

The mind is finally
clear.
Students shuffle
like mumbling ants
in a caravan of messy
little lives.
Should we be excited
or terrified?

There is little difference
now.
Only choice
and lack of
it.
One of ignorance,

sparkling with the rage
of pure conviction.
A riot
of the mind,
on your front lawn,
in The Capital.
Someone loses
their mind
in mass,
and we call on the gods
of exigent circumstance.
Maybe someone can explain us
to ourselves
Someday.

In Utero

Nothing exists
apart
from environment
- you, growing in my cocoon
fluttering daughter
The world must spin
so very different
for you
in your quiet, dark pool.

A warble, a muffle,
a murmur
and a whisper.
Is all we are to you
now.

Not for me to decide
the intention
of each creature.
Foreign and of unknown
origin, to you
holds no consequence
whether existence be of
ignorance
or bravery.

All is a flutter
- you spin
inside me
A universe
in a drop.

O untouchable, unfathomable
World.

Bible Thumper

One doesn't have to belt out
a masterpiece
to leave this world
satisfied
- Indeed,
only to sing
one perfect
note

A Quiet Power

A hundred quiet world
have lived and died
in my head.
Invisible pages
- unwritten stories,
love songs
unsung.
A heart left empty.

Share with me
my little lives:
detectives and lovesick
children, poems
in paintings, and paintings
in poems.

Love will never die
silent.
It will reach out
across the page
and leap
- electric
into the air,
melting, as sentiment

does
into the abyss
that is our time
on Earth.

First Snow

When you first saw
snow
your little hand
waved at the cold
air.

The frost on your
breath,
first ghost
on your lips,
and a life
brand new.

Tiny frozen
daubs
of little white
paint and your red
nose, my little Rudolph!
Mouth, agape
with wonder
and your beautiful eyes
sparkle
like I had never
believed
in a soul.

Marshmallows on the Moon

These are the rainbow years
This is the ocean
in one drop

This is you full
of giggles
and chocolate ice cream
torpedoing across multi-colored balls
in your pink, princess
tent.
These are the "ma ma ma" days
These are the "up so highs"

These are the cotton candy clouds
that cavort
with the waltzing bears.
This is eating marshmallows
on the moon.

Days with you
are days
of gentle dreams
of giggles and socks
of early mornings
and late nights

of baths and bare feet
of lullabies

These days
we don't stop to wonder
if the bear could actually
fit in the mitten.
It's your favorite book
and we just don't care.

Someday the future
will be the days
of quiet house
of broken hearts
and long goodbyes
of Easter waves
and grandchildren

But these are the days
of messy floors
of spaghetti on the ceiling
of dreaming dreams
of what you must be
dreaming.
Of rainbow years.
A world
in a life
in a small house.
The ocean

in a drop
and a love
that never
ends.

You are Family to Me

You are the embrace
of a hug.
You are family to me,
I will kiss
your tears away.
You are family
to me.

Whatever we do,
wherever we are
in my heart you'll always be.
With bubble baths
and kisses goodnight
more than all the stars
in the sky...
more than all the fish
in the sea...
mare than all of the numbers,
you are family to me.

When I look at the moon
or see friends
when we walk the block
or travel the world,

it's your world
I want to see.
Show me your light
and share it with me

.

There is no greater love
than for you, as you are
no wider reach
than this sea
whether in my smile
or the touch of my hand,
my love, you are family
to me

If Art can Save Us

We owe it to ourselves
to
try.

The Man I Love

Is the notebook by my
bedside table
- a private place
to put my joys
and my fears

The man I love
is an invisible circus
with starry nights
a roaring lion
and all life
set up taut
on a tightrope
we walk.
- No one said
this was going to be easy.

The man I love
is a quiet song
with a powerful ending.
A candle that burns
soft and slow.
A whisper in my ear
at night.

The man I love is a father
a dad
a stranger
and a friend.
He is a storm
of rabid
kisses,
or "I love you"s
gentle as
a lullaby

The man I love
is not
without his demons
He holds them
at bay
in a storm cloud
of the mind

The man I love has doubts
that he can be
the knight
on the white horse
the father that runs home
to us before the night
casts its warning
wail.
Doubts
that he can be

the man I love.

But he need not fear.
For when I close my eyes
it's him I see
frozen
in time
on a beach
in my mind
- dreams of Florida
flowers and eternal
sunshine
bare feet in the sand
and warm water washing
the shore.
He sees me in the distance,
baby girl in his arms
Our eyes meet:
we understand:
futures past and present
we share
both the real
and the imagined.

Man on a Bicycle: A Still Life with What we Carry

Any still life
will soon again
go fast.
Whether it takes a month
a day, or a minute.
Drop the pen,
click the shutter,
and the wheels spin,
and the man
disappears
on the horizon

Every still life
has invisible props
every smiling photo
every "girl with flowers"
"woman with dog"
"man with questions"
How are any of us enough
for any other
person
to love
to withstand
what we should have received

and didn't...
Enough to weather
the passage of time
and be for a child
what we still hope
to discover
for ourselves?

Into the distance
he rides
with his questions
and his
gentle
heart.
With his hope
and his love
and the goodness done
- soft hand,
crying head,
held low.
He is the man
who is there,
who withstands,
who endures,
who loves
who heals.

A strength and a passionate
wild

power
that pulls you
both into the dark
and through.

I Said "I Love You"

I said "I love you"
but should have said
I see in you
what others can't.
Walking Chicago at night
to take a homeless man
for a meal.
Music in the window
an endless summer
night
in Greek town.
An empty bed
and the taste of watermelon
and sweat still on my tongue.

I said "I love you"
but meant to say
that no one has ever
made me feel
so strong.
Paint dances
across canvas
words tempt me
on the page
and your late night ideas

I write down.
Anything is possible.
Anything
with you

I said I love you
but also,
I see you,
you are kind,
you are gracious,
and stronger
than you know
you are loved
and have been loved
by me.

Fruit Flies

Die engorging their bellies
on wine
when I met you
I was trapped
under a jar.
A hollow
knocking
under the ground
too polite
and easily ignored.
Entranced by the promise
to be loved
forever.

I have felt
detatched
from my face
.
Do you tell me
my insides
are ugly?
Do I believe every conspiracy
I read on the internet
that tells me
not to look

in abandoned baby
carriers?

The flies that lie
in the sill
have a life
base and short.
They are drawn
to the promise
of something
sweet
and bright...
but it is brief
and it is
dark
and they don't know
enough
to keep
from drowning
in it.

Love Story

Our love story
isn't perfect
But it's still
being written
One day
you will write me
a song
and I will paint
you and our baby
in so many colors
that will swirl
and entrance
your soul,
swinging you around
with glee
and you will see
the love that you are.

My Unicorn

The thing that you are
doesn't even know
what you are.
The touch of your hand
makes me
quiver.
In soft, wet
spaces.
A slippery eye, a hard
little mouth
waiting to receive
a kiss
on the back of
my neck, sends shivers
- pleasure
down my spine

The blue of your
eyes
makes me fall
and trust
you always.
strong arms
and tan
skin

I see the sun
in your hair
and your laugh
takes me home
to a family
of our own
and a whole world
made
together.

Loss

Death ends
a life,
not a relationship.
Living on
the wall, we swim
in pools
of the past
faces of our ancestors.

Sleeping on the mantle,
grandfather is layers
of stone,
hard and brave,
like the sword
he kept in the closet.
A promise to protect us
from intruders.

You live in the scent
of a fresh-picked
orange
and the dirt
beneath our roses.

You live
when a child
writes in broken
English, how each week,
he visits
the grave of his father,
and cries.

You live,
when I can read you
like a poem
- a mess of words,
scrambled and scribbled
in hieroglyphs, familiar
enough to make them mine.

Words, like a forgotten
face.

Exigent Circumstance

Exigent Circumstance

Dreams drone-hover
over a wasteland,
tumble weed
reality.
- The lingering storm
of grey matter
dancing across my cells.
The mind is finally
clear.

Students shuffle
as quiet as ants
in a caravan
of cars.
No one knows
whether to be excited
or terrified.
And choice,
the only difference
between them.
A gun shot,
a graduation,
a riot.

Doesn’t matter.
A large crowd
swarming with cell phones
is your only
lasting
evidence.

Conviction
or ignorance.
Doesn’t matter.
Both made with insidious,
exigent circumstance.
We all have reasons
for what we do
And
No one ever thinks
they are
a bad person.

Paint the Sky With Stars

I think that love
is something you
do
But it is also
some invisible
thing
that can happen inside
and nobody
knows.

For you, I will write
the stories
of star crossed
lovers
and poetry comes
in waves
of green.
I will paint
a landscape
on the inside
of your heart
and keep a place
by a soft
spring
just for us

-no one else
can see
this private painting
of the mind,
the carnival of my
soul

www.ingramcontent.com/pod-product-compliance
Lightning Source LLC
Chambersburg PA
CBHW051747130826
49812CB00033B/1038
9789357210423